S0-AFQ-758

Pink

Floyd

Other Titles in

Library Ed.
ISBN-13: 978-0-7660-3031-2
Paperback
ISBN-13: 978-0-7660-3623-9

Library Ed.
ISBN-13: 978-0-7660-3028-2
Paperback
ISBN-13: 978-0-7660-3620-8

Library Ed.
ISBN-13: 978-0-7660-3029-9
Paperback
ISBN-13: 978-0-7660-3621-5

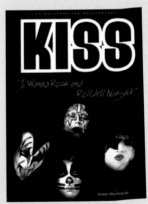

Library Ed.
ISBN-13: 978-0-7660-3027-5
Paperback
ISBN-13: 978-0-7660-3619-2

AN UNAUTHORIZED ROCKOGRAPHY

Pink Floyd

The Rock Band

Laura S. Jeffrey

REBELS OF ROCK

Enslow Publishers, Inc.
40 Industrial Road
Box 398
Berkeley Heights, NJ 07922
USA
http://www.enslow.com

Library of Congress Cataloging-in-Publication Data

Jeffrey, Laura S.
    Pink Floyd : the rock band / Laura S. Jeffrey.
        p. cm. — (Rebels of rock)
    Includes bibliographical references, discography, and index.
    Summary: "A biography of British rock band Pink Floyd"—Provided by publisher.
    ISBN-13: 978-0-7660-3030-5
    ISBN-10: 0-7660-3030-X
    1. Pink Floyd (Musical group)—Juvenile literature. 2. Rock musicians—England—Biography—
Juvenile literature. I. Title.
    ML3930.P47J44 2010
    782.42166'092—dc22
    [B]   2008017435

ISBN-13: 978-0-7660-3622-2 (paperback ed.)
ISBN-10: 0-7660-3622-7 (paperback ed.)

Printed in the United States of America

10 9 8 7 6 5 4 3 2 1

To Our Readers: This book has not been authorized by Pink Floyd or its successors.

We have done our best to make sure all Internet Addresses in this book were active and appropriate when we went to press. However, the author and the publisher have no control over and assume no liability for the material available on those Internet sites or on other Web sites they may link to. Any comments or suggestions can be sent by e-mail to comments@enslow.com or to the address on the back cover.

Every effort has been made to locate all copyright holders of material used in this book. If any errors or omissions have occurred, corrections will be made in future editions of this book.

♻ Enslow Publishers, Inc., is committed to printing our books on recycled paper. The paper in every book contains 10% to 30% post-consumer waste (PCW). The cover board on the outside of each book contains 100% PCW. Our goal is to do our part to help young people and the environment too!

Photo Credits: Associated Press, pp. 10, 36, 71, 80, 84; Ian Dickinson/Redferns, p. 27; EMI Archives/Redferns, p. 46; Everett Collection, pp. 53, 63, 74; Jill Furmanowsky/LFI, p. 29; Jill Furmanowsky/LFI-JF, p. 24; GAB Archives/Redferns, pp. 39, 41; Photo by Harry Goodwin/Rex Features/Courtesy Everett Collection, p. 31; © Pictorial Press Ltd/Alamy, p. 43; Photo by Brian Rasic/Rex Features/Courtesy Everett Collection, pp. 6, 12; Peter Still/Redferns, p. 61; WireImage/Getty Images, p. 16.

Cover Photo: Michael Ochs Archives/Getty Images

CONTENTS

David Gilmour, Roger Waters, Nick Mason, and Rick Wright performed together again as Pink Floyd during the 2005 Live 8 concerts.

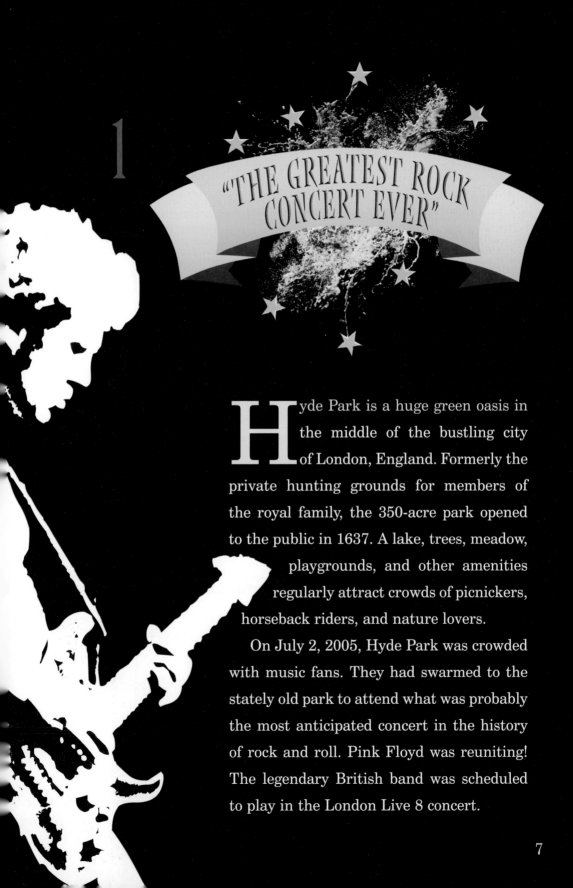

1

"THE GREATEST ROCK CONCERT EVER"

Hyde Park is a huge green oasis in the middle of the bustling city of London, England. Formerly the private hunting grounds for members of the royal family, the 350-acre park opened to the public in 1637. A lake, trees, meadow, playgrounds, and other amenities regularly attract crowds of picnickers, horseback riders, and nature lovers.

On July 2, 2005, Hyde Park was crowded with music fans. They had swarmed to the stately old park to attend what was probably the most anticipated concert in the history of rock and roll. Pink Floyd was reuniting! The legendary British band was scheduled to play in the London Live 8 concert.

Pink Floyd was formed by British schoolmates in the mid-1960s. The band quickly became renowned for its "psychedelic sound." It layered unusual sound effects over songs that featured intelligent lyrics, and melodies with classical music aspects. Pink Floyd was also renowned for elaborate stage shows. These performances simulated mind-altering experiences by using lights, sounds, films, and flying objects in creative ways. The group sold millions of records and remains one of the best-selling and critically acclaimed rock groups of all time. Yet even at the height of their popularity, Pink Floyd band members had remained somewhat mysterious. Album covers rarely featured photos of the band members. Instead, the covers were artistic representations of the songs' messages. Also, band members rarely gave interviews.

Pink Floyd members Roger Waters, David Gilmour, Nick Mason, and Rick Wright had performed together for almost fifteen years. The band had been the top act in their country's first multi-act, free rock concert, which was held in Hyde Park in June 1968. But then Wright, and then Waters, split from the group. Waters subsequently fought with Gilmour and Mason about whether they could call themselves "Pink Floyd" and continue making records without him.

Waters, Gilmour, Mason, and Wright had not performed together since 1981. Indeed, Waters had not even spoken to some of the band members in all those years. Yet for one night

only, at Live 8, the talented musicians had agreed to bury the bad feelings and perform together again.

Live 8 had been organized by Bob Geldof. The Irish punk rock musician was once the lead singer of the 1970s group the Boomtown Rats. Geldof had become a political activist after watching a television documentary about the famine in Ethiopia.

In 1984, Geldof wrote a song called "Do They Know It's Christmas?" He persuaded top British acts of the day to perform the song under the name Band Aid. The song raised millions of dollars for Ethiopia. The next year, Geldof organized Live Aid concerts in London and Philadelphia that raised even more money for famine relief.

Now, twenty years after Live Aid, Geldof was at it again. This time, he was not trying to raise money. Instead, Geldof said he simply wanted to raise awareness so that people all over the world would pressure their political leaders to help Africa. He believed lawmakers should cancel billions of dollars in African debt, increase aid to Africa by at least $50 billion, and rewrite trade regulations to be more favorable to Africa as well as poor countries.[1]

To those skeptics who did not believe that concerts could actually help Africa, Geldof said, "Mahatma Gandhi freed a continent, Martin Luther King freed a people, Nelson Mandela freed a country. It does work—they [political leaders] will listen."[2]

MANY MUSICIANS PERFORMED DURING LIVE 8, INCLUDING
STEVIE WONDER.

Geldof designed Live 8 as a series of concerts. They
would take place in ten cities around the globe, including
Philadelphia, Pennsylvania; Tokyo, Japan; Berlin, Germany;
and Paris, France. Also, the Live 8 concerts would feature performances by the biggest names in the music industry. They
included country singers Faith Hill and Tim McGraw; pop
stars Celine Dion, Destiny's Child, Madonna, and Mariah
Carey; singer-songwriters Stevie Wonder and Alicia Keys;
Latin singer Shakira; Italian tenor Andrea Bocelli; rappers
Jay-Z, Snoop Dogg, Kanye West, and Will Smith; and bands

Coldplay, Green Day, Audioslave, Maroon 5, Linkin Park, REM, Good Charlotte, and Black Eyed Peas. Live 8 was not only destined to be the biggest musical concert of its time but also, as Geldof said, "the greatest rock concert ever."[3]

Geldof had scheduled Live 8 to take place during the Group of Eight, or G-8, Summit. This annual meeting brings together the leaders of eight powerful nations—Canada, France, Germany, Italy, Japan, Russia, the United Kingdom, and the United States—to talk about issues of global importance. Leaders from other nations and organizations are often invited to join the regular attendees. In 2005, the United Kingdom was hosting the G-8 summit in Gleneagles, Scotland.

Geldof had persuaded all the musicians to play for free so that concertgoers would not be required to purchase tickets. It was estimated that up to a billion people of all ages, races, and nationalities attended the concerts, heard them on satellite radio, and watched televised broadcasts and live Internet streams.

"It's great to be asked to help [Geldof] raise public awareness on the issues of Third World debt and poverty," Waters told reporters before the concert. "Also, to be given the opportunity to put the band back together, even if it's only for a few numbers, is a big bonus."[4]

More than two hundred thousand people swarmed to Hyde Park for the London Live 8 concert. They were the lucky winners of a lottery to determine who would receive free tickets to the concert. Paul McCartney opened the eight-hour show. He was joined by Bono and U2 in a rendition of the Beatles hit "Sgt. Pepper's Lonely Hearts Club Band." The London lineup also included Annie Lennox, George Michael, and Sting. Lennox had been lead singer of the Eurythmics, and Michael had been half of the duo Wham! Sting had been lead singer of the rock band Police.

The show was going very well, but it was running behind schedule. It was not until about 11:00 P.M. that finally, Pink

PINK FLOYD PERFORMED FOUR SONGS. MANY FANS WONDERED IF THE BAND WAS GETTING BACK TOGETHER.

Floyd took the darkened stage. They opened with the song "Speak to Me/Breathe." Drummer Nick Mason later said that he had been feeling anxious and excited, with adrenaline "bubbling underneath while nervousness crept stealthily in."[5] However, "once the tape of the heartbeat for 'Breathe' started in the pitch black arena I was already relaxing, easing into being part of a band."[6]

To the cheers, whistles, and applause of the excited and appreciative crowd, Waters, Gilmour, Mason, and Wright performed. Their repertoire for that evening included "Money" and "Comfortably Numb." "The aging giants of psychedelic rock not only sounded superb . . . they seemed genuinely happy to be together again," *Chicago Sun-Times* music reviewer Jim DeRogatis wrote after the concert.[7]

The Pink Floyd musicians ended their four-song set with a group hug. But perhaps the most touching moment came as the band struck the opening notes to their haunting and melodic song "Wish You Were Here."

"It's quite emotional standing up here with these three guys after all these years, standing to be counted with the rest of you," Waters told the crowd. "Anyway, we're doing this for everyone who's not here but particularly, of course, for Syd."[8]

Who was Syd? As longtime fans of the band knew, Syd was Roger "Syd" Barrett, Waters's childhood friend and former classmate. It was Barrett who started the band, and Barrett who came up with the name "Pink Floyd." It was

Barrett who wrote Pink Floyd's first three singles and most of the songs on the band's heralded first album, *The Piper at the Gates of Dawn*. And it was Barrett who had deeply influenced the group's later recordings. Indeed, to many fans, Barrett *was* Pink Floyd.

But Barrett had left the group—he was kicked out, actually, though he may not have understood what was going on—before Pink Floyd had realized its greatest successes. His drug abuse reportedly led to mental illness, and he had become unreliable and uncommunicative. Barrett wound up leaving the music business altogether. Indeed, he practically dropped out of life itself. He had spent the last two decades living as a recluse, with very little contact with the outside world.

"I'm very sad about Syd," Waters once said. "Of course he was important and the band would never have . . . started without him because he was writing all the material. It couldn't have happened without him but on the other hand it couldn't have gone on with him."9

Waters, Gilmour, Mason, and Wright had thought about asking Barrett to join them for the Live 8 reunion. Those who knew Barrett best believed that even if the offer had been extended, Barrett would have said no.

"I saw him this morning and told him [about the concert], but he did not react," said Barrett's sister

Rosemary. "That is another life for him, another world in another time."[10]

Another life, another world, another time—and another person. Syd Barrett was a creative genius who drew on his middle-class English childhood, and combined his love of art and music, to launch what would become a legendary band. But it would become a legend without him.

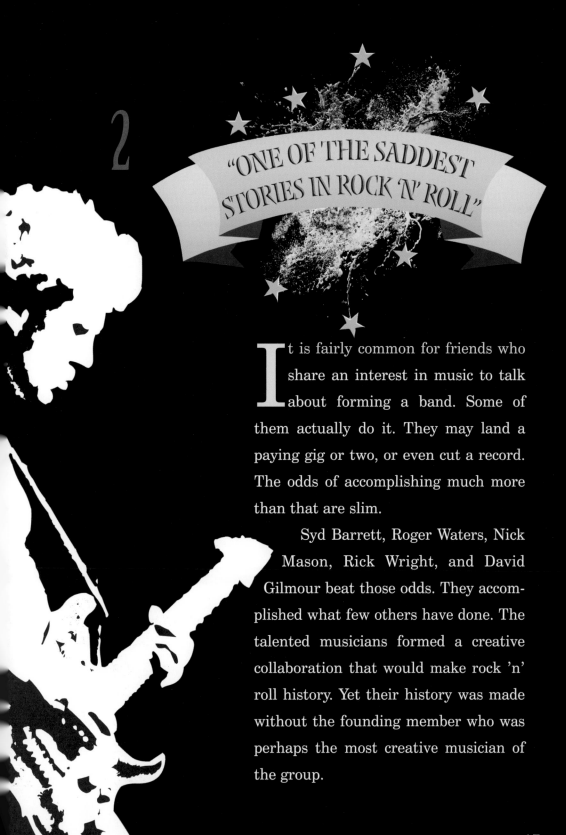

2

It is fairly common for friends who share an interest in music to talk about forming a band. Some of them actually do it. They may land a paying gig or two, or even cut a record. The odds of accomplishing much more than that are slim.

Syd Barrett, Roger Waters, Nick Mason, Rick Wright, and David Gilmour beat those odds. They accomplished what few others have done. The talented musicians formed a creative collaboration that would make rock 'n' roll history. Yet their history was made without the founding member who was perhaps the most creative musician of the group.

Syd Barrett

Brilliant, creative, witty, and friendly. Vacant, confused, violent, and reclusive. All of these adjectives are used to describe Roger "Syd" Barrett, founder of Pink Floyd and the band's source of inspiration for its greatest hits. While the adjectives paint a contradictory picture of the talented man, those who know him say he was a different person before he was forever changed by drugs. His wasted talent is a chilling reminder of how dangerous drugs are.

"If he hadn't had this complete nervous breakdown, he could easily have been one of the greatest songwriters today," said Pink Floyd keyboard player Rick Wright. "I think it's one of the saddest stories in rock 'n' roll, what happened to Syd. He was brilliant—and such a nice guy."[1]

Roger Keith "Syd" Barrett was born in Cambridge, England, on January 6, 1946. He was the fourth of five children born to Dr. Arthur and Winifred Barrett. Dr. Barrett was a pathologist who was also very interested in music and art. He painted watercolors and was a member of the Cambridge Philharmonic Society.[2]

Like his father, Syd developed interests in music and art. When Syd was a teenager, his parents bought him an acoustic guitar. He taught himself how to play, and often had friends over to his house for impromptu jam sessions. Later, he and his friends formed bands and performed in local nightclubs. It was during these years that he picked up the nickname Syd.

When Syd was fifteen, his father died. Around this time, Syd also began experimenting with marijuana. "Syd was someone who, despite being very gregarious on the surface, had a very secret side," said a friend from his teen years. "There was a part of him you could never reach."[3]

Barrett attended Cambridge High School for Boys, and then Cambridge College of Arts and Technology. In November 1963, he was planning to attend a Beatles concert, but had to miss it to interview for a spot at the Camberwell School of Art in London. Barrett received a scholarship to the school and moved to London in 1964.

He was a "very charming fellow, with a lightness and a sparkle about his personality that was uplifting," said Mike Leonard. Leonard was an architecture professor who rented a house to Barrett and some friends. Leonard also said Barrett was "always playing with words."[4]

"Syd was very good looking and had this sort of mad attractiveness about him," said one of his girlfriends, Gala Pinion. "He had the most extraordinary eyes and when he looked at you, you felt hopelessly caught."[5]

After Barrett moved to London, he began writing songs, putting a band together—and taking more drugs. Barrett was "always experimenting" and had a "very open sort of mind . . . to an almost dangerous degree," his friends recalled.[6]

Lysergic acid diethylamide, or LSD, was Barrett's drug of choice. LSD is a powerful drug that causes hallucinations, which are distortions in a person's perception of reality. Users see, hear, and feel things that seem real but are not. These "trips" can be pleasant, confusing, or even horrifying. Also, they can last for several hours.

The effects of LSD are unpredictable. They depend on the amount of the drug that was taken as well as the user's personality and mood.[7] LSD users sometimes experience flashbacks, or reminders of the trip, without taking the drug again. These flashbacks can occur for more than a year after LSD use. LSD can also trigger long-lasting mental illnesses such as schizophrenia or severe depression.[8] This is particularly true for people who have a family history of mental illness.

Barrett wrote most of the songs on the first Pink Floyd album, *The Piper at the Gates of Dawn*. One friend recalled that Barrett believed his art and music complemented each other. "He was always trying to get his music to sound like his art and vice versa," this friend said.[9]

Perhaps Barrett felt that LSD opened up his creative side; perhaps he took drugs to escape the pressure of success. But Barrett underwent a drastic change in 1967. That was the year *Gates of Dawn* was released; Barrett was twenty-one years old.

"It was very sad," said music producer Joe Boyd. He worked with Pink Floyd on the group's first single, "Arnold Layne." "I liked Syd a lot. He was a very bright guy, and one

of the things about him was he had these sparkling dark eyes and you know, girls loved him."[10]

Drugs had taken their toll; Barrett left the band. His last show with Pink Floyd was in January 1968. The band had just started recording its second album, *A Saucerful of Secrets*. By this time, Barrett was largely uncommunicative and often violent.

After Barrett left Pink Floyd, he received psychiatric care and seemed to do better for awhile. He also released two solo albums in 1970, *The Madcap Laughs* and *Barrett*. He had help from Pink Floyd band mates David Gilmour and Roger Waters, among others.

"Listening to the [songs] that he released when he was messed up . . . they are wonderfully playful and still in the spirit [of the times]," said Frank Felice, an associate professor of music.[11] Felice teaches an honors seminar on Pink Floyd at Butler University in Indianapolis, Indiana. He said Barrett's song "Effervescing Elephant" is "just one of the most wonderful, silly pieces of music ever." Also, Barrett's songs "Scream the Last Scream" and "Vegetable Man" show "a great sense of creativity, even though it's incredibly unhinged," Felice said.[12]

At the time of their release, reviewers were divided in their praise of Barrett's albums. However, the albums no doubt showed to the world how sick Barrett had become. The albums included Barrett's nervous coughs, shuffling of pages, and cries of frustration when asked to do another take.[13]

"Perhaps we were trying to show what Syd was really like," said Gilmour, who helped produce the album. "But perhaps we were trying to punish him."[14]

"His second album has fantastic moments," wrote one reviewer. However, "on several tracks he really sounds, for better or worse, like a man who has gone quite mad."[15]

At the time, Barrett was dating Gala Pinion. They moved into his mother's home in Cambridge, and the couple became engaged. Barrett continued to use drugs, however, and he reportedly became very violent at times. The couple broke up and Pinion moved out.

Barrett tried to put another band together and record a third album, but his efforts failed. He spent more time in a psychiatric hospital. Gradually, he withdrew from friends and family. By this time, Pink Floyd had released three additional albums, and Barrett had become a legend in England. Loyal fans camped out outside his mother's home. Trying to escape the attention, Barrett moved to an apartment in London in 1972. He lived there for eight years, rarely leaving home.

Barrett had violent episodes and compulsively bought guitars and television sets, only to give them away. He shaved his head and gained a lot of weight. "I don't know what he's like in his head because he does not talk at all," Pink Floyd keyboardist Wright told an interviewer on Montreal Radio. "It's very sad. He can't relate to anyone."[16]

In 1980, Barrett moved back to his mother's house

in Cambridge. Winifred Barrett died in 1991, but Barrett continued to live in the home. Though still a recluse and in poor health, he seemingly was at peace. "He's not mentally OK, but he gets by," Pink Floyd guitarist David Gilmour said in 1994. "He manages, he lives, he takes his clothes to the Laundromat to get them cleaned. I'm actually very tempted to visit him. He was a wonderful talent and friend."[17]

Fans continued to try to track Barrett down. Rumors swirled about his whereabouts and state of mind. Reporters tried to interview him. But Barrett's family made it clear that the burned-out musician—who by now had returned to his given name of Roger—wanted to be left alone.

Roger Waters

The other members of Pink Floyd were not only band mates to Syd Barrett. They were also his childhood friends, classmates, and roommates. Bass guitarist and vocalist George Roger Waters was born on September 6, 1943, in Great Bookham, England. He was the youngest of two sons born to Eric Fletcher Waters and his wife, Mary Waters. Eric Fletcher Waters was a member of the British air force fighting in World War II. Just a few months after Roger was born, his father was killed in action in the battle of Anzio, Italy. Mary Waters was a piano teacher. One of her students was Syd Barrett, who became friends with Roger.

Roger reportedly had unhappy experiences in school.

Roger Waters
in the 1970s

He would later call on those experiences to write the lyrics for what would become some of the most memorable Pink Floyd songs. As a teenager, Roger took an interest in music. Yet after graduating from Cambridge High School for Boys, he enrolled at Regent Street Polytechnic School in London in 1962 to study architecture. Waters rented a house from an architecture professor. Barrett, his childhood buddy, was in London studying art. They became roommates for awhile. Waters soon grew more interested in music than in architecture, and he often jammed with Barrett and other friends. Waters taught himself bass guitar since Barrett was a better guitarist.

After Barrett left Pink Floyd, Waters became the band's main lyricist. His sources of inspiration included the friend he had lost to drugs and mental illness, and the heroic father he never knew.

Waters is also interested in classical music and politics. He wrote an opera based on the French Revolution, and he has written songs to express his displeasure over the war in Iraq. Waters is also involved in charitable groups including Millennium Promise, which is working to erase poverty.

Waters has been described as domineering and having a big ego. In fact, it was Waters's ego that was blamed for much of the problems among Pink Floyd band members.

"He could not tolerate anyone else having any real say in what was going on," said guitarist David Gilmour.[18] Drummer

Nick Mason said, "It was a case of either convince everyone else or make everyone do what you want to do."[19]

Waters has been married four times and has three children.

David Gilmour

Guitarist David Jon Gilmour was born on March 6, 1946, in Cambridge, England. He was the second of four children born to Douglas Gilmour, a professor of zoology, and Sylvia, a teacher and film editor.

Gilmour attended Perse Preparatory School for Boys in Cambridge and then Cambridge College of Arts and Technology, where he met Syd Barrett. Gilmour and Barrett often played their guitars during class breaks. They also spent a summer together hitchhiking throughout France.

Gilmour was studying languages in college but inspired by a Bob Dylan album, he dropped out at the age of eighteen to pursue a music career.[20] He was in several bands that played at military bases and toured throughout Europe. Gilmour also earned money modeling. He joined Pink Floyd in January 1968, when it became clear to the other band members that they needed help because of Barrett's state of mind.

Gilmour is a songwriter, vocalist, and guitarist. He is best known for playing the Stratocaster model of electric guitar, but he also plays the acoustic guitar and piano. Recently, he learned how to play the saxophone. He has an extensive

David Gilmour in 1977

guitar collection and bought the first Fender Stratocaster ever made.[21]

Gilmour has also taken an interest in the careers of other musicians. He helped teenager Kate Bush land a record contract in the 1970s; Bush's debut album became a best-seller. Gilmour is also involved in charities including Crisis, a London-based organization to help the homeless. Gilmour has been married twice and has seven children.

Nick Mason

Drummer Nicholas Berkeley "Nick" Mason was born on January 27, 1944, in Birmingham, England, to Bill and Sally Mason. Bill Mason directed documentary films. As a child, Nick took piano and violin lessons, but he was not really interested in either instrument. However, when he was thirteen, he acquired his first album. It was an Elvis Presley record. Nick became intrigued with the idea of joining a band and playing music with his friends. He asked for money for Christmas and bought himself a drum kit, then taught himself how to play.

"Every kid should be in a band," Mason once said. "It's great to play music, but even better to understand the necessity of working together to get the result . . . and it's a lot less arduous than football."[22]

Like Roger Barrett and Rick Wright, Mason studied architecture at Regent Street Polytechnic School. He enrolled in 1962. "I was certainly interested in [architecture], but not

Nick Mason
in the 1970s

particularly committed to it as a career," Mason recalled. "Despite my lack of burning ambition, the course offered a variety of disciplines—including fine art, graphics and technology—which proved to deliver a good all-round education, and which probably explains why Roger, Rick and I all . . . shared an enthusiasm for the possibilities offered by technology and visual effects."[23]

"In later years we would become heavily involved in everything from the construction of lighting towers to album cover artwork and studio and stage design," Mason said. "Our architectural training allowed us the luxury of making relatively informed comments whenever we brought the real experts in."[24]

Auto racing is a favorite hobby of Mason's. He owns and races several classic cars. He is also a pilot. Mason has been married twice and has four children.

Richard "Rick" Wright

Keyboardist Richard William "Rick" Wright was born in London, England, on July 28, 1943. He was one of three children born to Cedric and Bridie Wright. Like Roger Waters and Nick Mason, Wright was a student at Regent Street Polytechnic. He studied architecture and music. Wright had learned to play piano, harmonium, harpsichord, and cello before enrolling in college. He had also developed an interest in electronic compositions.[25]

Rick Wright
in 1967

Along with playing keyboard and piano, Wright also sang background vocals and some lead vocals for Pink Floyd. He is probably the least known of the Pink Floyd band members because he rarely gives interviews. He has also been called the "unsung hero" of the band, meaning his contributions have been overlooked. Wright has been married three times and has three children.

As young boys growing up in England, Syd Barrett, Roger Waters, Nick Mason, Rick Wright, and David Gilmour shared an interest in music. When they grew older and began to collaborate, the result was magic.

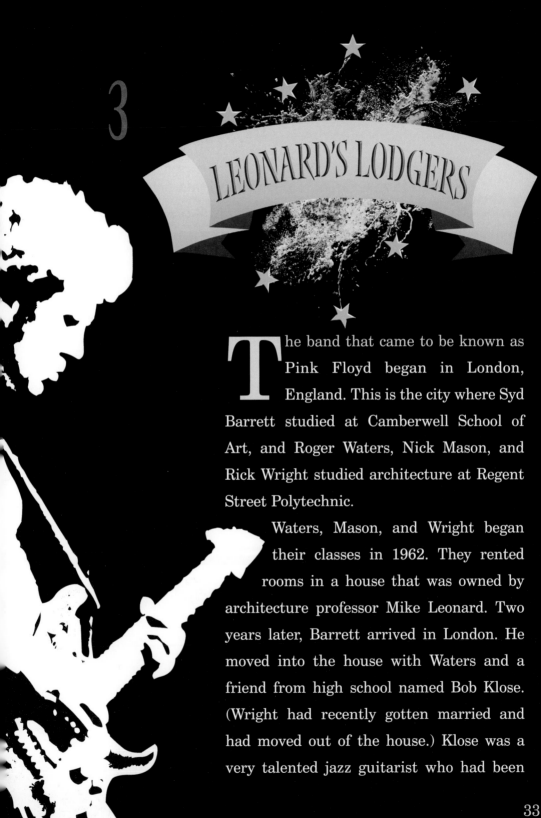

3

LEONARD'S LODGERS

T he band that came to be known as Pink Floyd began in London, England. This is the city where Syd Barrett studied at Camberwell School of Art, and Roger Waters, Nick Mason, and Rick Wright studied architecture at Regent Street Polytechnic.

Waters, Mason, and Wright began their classes in 1962. They rented rooms in a house that was owned by architecture professor Mike Leonard. Two years later, Barrett arrived in London. He moved into the house with Waters and a friend from high school named Bob Klose. (Wright had recently gotten married and had moved out of the house.) Klose was a very talented jazz guitarist who had been

33

playing with a band in Cambridge, England. He had decided to put music on hold to study architecture.

With Mason on drums and Barrett, Waters, and Klose on guitars, the roommates began jamming in the basement of Leonard's house for fun. They called themselves Leonard's Lodgers. "You could hear them when you turned off the main road a quarter of a mile away," Leonard said. "The noise was phenomenal."[1]

Leonard liked what he heard, and he encouraged his tenants to get paying gigs. The roommates asked Wright to join their band as keyboardist. They tapped an older acquaintance named Chris Dennis to be lead singer. Dennis was in the Royal Air Force and played music on the side.

"We'd go out and do 10 pound [dollar] gigs and play at people's parties," Waters said, "and we bought some gear and gradually got a bit more involved."[2] The group's early shows consisted mainly of covering songs of musicians who were popular at the time, including Bo Diddley, Muddy Waters, and Chuck Berry.

One day, Barrett was looking through some old blues albums. He came across records by noted musicians Pink Anderson and Floyd Council. Barrett combined their first two names and presented it to his friends as the new band name. A few years later, Barrett told interviewers that the name "Pink Floyd" had been transmitted to him from a flying saucer.

Chris Dennis ended his relationship with Pink Floyd when the Air Force transferred him to the Persian Gulf in January 1965. As the year progressed, Barrett focused his creative energy on music instead of art. He grew more confident of his singing, and he started writing songs. He listened to records from the Mothers of Invention, the Byrds, and the Kinks. He read books including *Grimm's Fairy Tales*, *The Hobbit*, *Lord of the Rings*, and *The Wind in the Willows*. All of these influenced his songs, which combined rhythm and blues, improvisations on guitar and keyboards, mystical imagery, and witty reflections on British life.

Barrett also played around with different sounds to layer over the music. "[Leonard] had these gongs and electronic devices in the attic and Syd used to experiment with the various noises," a friend recalled years later. "I guess that was how he worked out the early Floyd sound."[3]

Barrett's new direction for the band did not agree with Klose, who preferred a more traditional style. Also, Klose's parents were worried that music was interfering with their son's studies. So by the summer of 1965, Klose told his roommates he was quitting the band. He left on friendly terms.

Waters and Mason spent that summer working in architecture firms, but Barrett traveled to France. There, he met up with David Gilmour, who was playing guitar in a band called Joker's Wild. They traveled and played music together. Barrett also kept a notebook and jotted down ideas for songs.

In early 1967, Pink Floyd landed a deal with EMI Records. Here, they jump from the steps of EMI House in London.

When Barrett returned to London, he continued on his creative streak and wrote several songs. "Through the whimsy and crazy juxtaposition of ideas and words, there was a very powerful grasp of humanity," Waters said of Barrett's songs. "They were quintessentially human songs."[4]

Throughout the fall of 1965 and into 1966, Pink Floyd landed gigs at parties, clubs, and colleges. They became regulars at UFO, a London nightclub that featured unknown bands performing cutting-edge music.

Pink Floyd no longer just covered popular songs. The band also played Barrett's compositions. Instead of playing the songs straight, they improvised and added unusual sounds. During one show, for example, Barrett strummed his guitar strings with a metal cigarette lighter. *Guitar Player* magazine later said the technique produced a sound like "whooping, seagull-like cries."[5]

"I think concerts have given us a chance to realize that maybe the music we play isn't directed at dancing, necessarily, like normal pop groups," Barrett once said.[6]

"When the Floyd played it was very exciting," said The Who's guitarist Pete Townshend. "Their sound fitted that period with echo on all the instruments. I once got Eric Clapton to come down [to UFO] because I thought what Syd was doing was very interesting." Townshend noted that Barrett set up the amplifiers so that each played a different sound. He said what Barrett did "was not always melodically or harmonically correct but always very interesting and satisfying."[7]

Pink Floyd's performances also incorporated lights and images shown from a projector. They came to be known as a "psychedelic band" and attracted a lot of attention. At one show, more than twenty-five hundred people crammed into the venue to watch Pink Floyd and others perform.

Not all of the publicity Pink Floyd received was positive, however. A British newspaper reporter wrote a story that said psychedelic rock glorified drug use, and that many of the psychedelic musicians were using drugs. That was certainly true for Barrett. He was taking LSD. However, Barrett once said his Pink Floyd band mates were "dead straight," meaning they did not take drugs or approve of his drug use.[8]

By the end of February 1967, Pink Floyd went into the studio to record a single. The band hoped the single would entice a record company to sign them to a contract to produce an entire album. The A-side of the single was "Arnold Layne." This was a song Barrett wrote about a man who steals women's underwear from clotheslines. It was based on a true story. The song was considered very controversial for its time, and Radio London banned it from airplay. On the B-side was another Barrett composition, "Candy and a Currant Bun." This song was originally titled "Let's Roll Another," which referred to a marijuana cigarette. Music producers told

Barrett to rewrite the song to take out the references to drugs and sex.

Despite being banned from the radio, "Arnold Layne" made it onto the British Top 20 list, and Pink Floyd landed a record deal with EMI Records. The band performed their hit on the British TV show *Top of the Pops* and staged several more concerts in area clubs. They also began recording their first album. In May 1967, Pink Floyd released a second single, "See Emily Play." This, too, was written by Barrett, and reached the British Top 20.

Soon, people close to the band would wonder if they had put too much pressure on the twenty-one-year-old Barrett to write hit songs. For while the band's career was taking off, bad things were happening with Barrett. His LSD use had escalated, and it was feared that the drug had triggered mental illness.

"The pressures which hit him were the pressures from going from just being another guy on the block to being the spokesman for your generation," said Peter Jenner, who was one of Pink

IN 1967, PINK FLOYD RELEASED "SEE EMILY PLAY."

Floyd's managers and producers. "People would come up and ask him the meaning of life—that put a young person who'd just written a song and played a bit of guitar under enormous pressure."[9]

"Up until the spring of '67 he was charming, impish and witty," said Joe Boyd, the record producer who worked with the band on "Arnold Layne." "However, when I saw him that June [1967], he had gone through a dramatic deterioration, and he was almost monosyllabic and very blank-faced."[10]

"Syd was having good days and bad days," said Pink Floyd drummer Nick Mason, "and the bad days seemed to be increasing in number."[11]

Barrett became more and more unreliable. He arrived late for gigs, and walked offstage in the middle of songs. During some performances, he stood in place and simply played one chord over and over. Other times, he detuned his guitar in the middle of a performance.

There were also difficulties during the recording of the group's first album. "There are no pleasant memories," said EMI staff producer Norman Smith. "I always left with a headache. Syd was undisciplined: he would never sing the same thing twice. Trying to talk to him was like talking to a brick wall, because his face was so expressionless."[12]

Barrett's old friend David Gilmour recalled that Barrett invited him to visit Abbey Road Studios, where Pink Floyd was recording. (Coincidentally, the Beatles were also there working on *Sgt. Pepper's Lonely Hearts Club Band*.) "And I went down there and he didn't even recognize me," Gilmour said.[13]

Another time, Barrett "freaked out" after learning the band was scheduled for another appearance on *Top of the Pops*, and he walked out of a recording session. "That really was the first sign of his complete mental breakdown," producer Richard Buskin said. "And he never did come back into the studio after that, meaning that I had a . . . hard time with the recordings."[14]

Pink Floyd's first album, *The Piper at the Gates of Dawn*, was released in August 1967. The album title is borrowed from a line in the classic book *The Wind in the Willows*. The album cover featured photos of the band members on the front cover, one of the few Pink Floyd albums to do so. The album was well received in the United Kingdom. However, it was relatively unknown in the United States.

Barrett, Waters, Mason, and Wright all shared the writing credit

A CONCERT POSTER FROM 1967 SHOWS WHEN PINK FLOYD WOULD HAVE PLAYED IN CALIFORNIA AT THE WINTERLAND BALLROOM. THE CONCERT WAS CANCELED BECAUSE OF SYD BARRETT'S UNUSUAL BEHAVIOR.

for "Interstellar Overdrive," a ten-minute-long instrumental song that was one of the first psychedelic improvisations. But Barrett wrote most of the other songs on the album, including "Astronomy Domine," "Lucifer Sam," and "Bike." He also sang lead vocals or shared vocals with Waters and Wright on all but one song.

By the time the album was released, Barrett had become impossible to deal with. He showed up at interviews wearing filthy clothing. He disappeared for long periods of time. His behavior forced Pink Floyd to cancel a tour through Germany to promote the album. Then, in October, the band traveled to the United States but cut the tour after just one week. Barrett refused to sing or play his guitar during tapings of Dick Clark's *American Bandstand*. During an appearance on The *Pat Boone Show*, he just stared at Boone when Boone asked him questions.

"The rest of us were finally reaching our breaking point," said Mason. "We had tried to ignore the problems, and willed them to go away, but even our lust to succeed could no longer obscure the fact that we could not continue with Syd in this state . . . .it just was not fun anymore—and doubtless no fun for Syd either."[15]

The band had started working on a second album, and Mason, Waters, and Wright realized they needed help. In December 1967, they contacted David Gilmour. He was Barrett's high school friend, one-time traveling companion—

IN 1968, PINK FLOYD PERFORMED IN NEW YORK. ROGER WATERS IS PLAYING BASS AND NICK MASON IS PLAYING DRUMS.

and an excellent guitarist who had experience playing in a band. Gilmour's band, Joker's Wild, had broken up, and Gilmour was looking for a new gig. He was a quick study, and he sounded a lot like Barrett when he sang. Gilmour also was able to learn all the Pink Floyd songs in a few days.

Waters, Mason, and Wright told Gilmour that they did not want to replace Barrett. They simply needed to supplement him. Barrett would continue to write songs, but Gilmour would play lead guitar and sing vocals on recordings and in concerts.

"My initial ambition was just to get the band into some sort of shape," Gilmour said years later. "It seems ridiculous now, but I thought the band was awfully bad at the time when I joined. The gigs I'd seen with Syd were incredibly undisciplined. The lead figure was falling apart, and so was the band."[16]

Gilmour's first appearance with Pink Floyd was on January 12, 1968. For the next few weeks, all five musicians played in Pink Floyd shows. However, "Syd wasn't doing anything," recalled one person close to the group. "He was just sitting on the front of the stage, kicking his legs. It was very, very odd."[17]

"What Syd was experiencing at these shows we can only guess at," Mason said. "He was probably completely confused, and angry that his influence was being steadily eroded. . . . As he withdrew further and further, this merely convinced us that we were taking the right decision."[18]

Barrett's final performance with Pink Floyd was January 20, 1968. He had become so useless that in early February, his band mates simply decided not to pick him up for the next gig. As they were driving to the show, "Someone said, 'Shall we pick up Syd?'" Gilmour recalled. "And someone else said, 'Nah, let's not bother.' And that was the end."[19]

Pink Floyd's second album, *A Saucerful of Secrets*, was released in June 1968. Already, the band had been compensating for Barrett's absence. Barrett contributed only one song to

"Let There Be More Light," "Set the Controls for the Heart of the Sun," and "Corporal Clegg." Rick Wright wrote two songs: "Remember a Day" and "See-Saw." Wright also sang lead vocals on most of the songs. And Waters, Wright, Gilmour, and Mason shared writing credit for the instrumental song for which the album was named. *A Saucerful of Secrets* reached the number nine spot on the record charts in the United Kingdom, but it did not sell well in the United States.

The Pink Floyd members had hoped that Barrett could continue with the group in some capacity. It quickly became apparent that he could not. As the 1960s gave way to a new decade, Barrett descended into mental illness. Waters, Mason, Wright, and Gilmour realized that the new Pink Floyd would have to make its own way, without its founder and former front man.

By 1968, Pink Floyd was back to four members, from left to right: Rick Wright, David Gilmour, Roger Waters, and Nick Mason.

4

A GOOD TIME FOR ROCK

The musicians of Pink Floyd came of age during the 1960s. The decade was marked by experimentation, rebellion, creativity—and really great music. It was also a time when many young adults questioned authority and chose to act against social norms and customs. The music of the times reflected this.

A number of the British bands that were established in the 1960s are now considered legendary. During this ten-year period, the Beatles released their first single, became an international sensation, and broke up. Mick Jagger and Keith Richards joined forces with Charlie Watts, Brian Jones, and Bill Wyman and became the Rolling Stones. Eric Clapton moved from one now-classic group, Cream, to another, the Yardbirds, before setting out on a hugely successful solo career. Brothers Ray and Dave Davies formed the Kinks.

Then there was Pink Floyd. The so-called "psychedelic rockers" combined music with patterns, objects, lights, and sound to provide concertgoers with more than just an auditory experience. It was a concert to appeal to all the senses. In fact, Pink Floyd is believed to be the first British rock band to use a light show as part of its act.[1] The group developed a following in the London rock "underground scene" because their concerts combined unusual sound effects with light shows, as well as musical compositions that sometimes lasted for ten or more minutes. The group appealed to a younger generation looking for different answers and new ways of looking at things.

"When Syd left the band we did lose some of our credibility with 'the underground,'" recalled Nick Mason. "There . . . is a school of thought that Syd's departure marked the end of the 'real' Pink Floyd."[2]

"Syd was so deified that when he left the band, there was a whole lot of people who stopped listening to Pink Floyd, because they thought that Pink Floyd didn't exist any longer,"[3] said Frank Felice. Felice is a music professor who teaches a course on the rock band at Butler University in Indianapolis, Indiana.

With guitarist David Gilmour's arrival in 1968, Pink Floyd

did change. After all, Barrett had been the main songwriter and lead singer. But bass guitarist Roger Waters and keyboardist Rick Wright started writing more and taking over lead vocals. And the experienced and capable Gilmour enhanced the other band members' efforts. "They really needed someone like David Gilmour," said Keith Clifton, a Pink Floyd fan and associate professor at Central Michigan University School of Music. "He was not only incredibly gifted as a guitarist, but also as an overall musician that really moved the band forward."[4]

"David Gilmour, I'd say he's another one of those musicians who's really notable as much as anything for the sound he gets," said Steve Waksman, who wrote the book *Instruments of Desire: The Electric Guitar and the Shaping of the Musical Experience*. "This is kind of a hypnotic effect that Gilmour has."[5]

"When I heard that Syd had left the group, I thought they would disappear," said record producer Joe Boyd. "But in fact they went from strength to strength."[6]

Gradually, the band developed a more structured sound. As Mason recalled, the song "Careful With That Axe, Eugene" is more complex than typical songs of the time. "That complexity may have only been, 'quiet, loud, quiet, loud again,'" he said. "But at a time when most rock bands only had two volume settings—painfully loud and really, really, painfully loud—this was groundbreaking stuff."[7]

Bjorn Berkhout is a music professor at Loyola University in Chicago. He said Barrett's legacy "permeates everything the band did" after he left the group. "But at the same time, they moved away from what Barrett would have been with the group," he said. "They developed a unique, post-Syd Barrett Pink Floyd. But they would not have been what they were if it was not for Syd Barrett."[8]

"It's very hard to analyze what makes things work," Gilmour said. "We had Rick, who wasn't a very driven person, but had a very good musical brain; he would sit and plonk away, and a lot of the time he would play very beautiful pieces. Roger had fantastic drive, and a very good brain for lyrics. He was a very driving, creative force."[9]

Pink Floyd also began trying out new things technically and artistically. The group "tended to be a little bit more experimental in terms of the way that they put songs together," said Clifton. "A lot of their songs are in unusual meters—you know, not just the typical four-beat patterns. They were really very much ahead of their time."[10]

The group also became involved in writing music for avant-garde films. From 1968 to 1972, Pink Floyd wrote the soundtracks for four such movies.

In 1969, Pink Floyd band members created a 360-degree stereo system. The purpose was "to throw away the old format of the pop show—standing on a square stage at one end of a rectangular room and running through a series of numbers,"

Waters said. "Our idea is to put the sound all around with ourselves in the middle. Then the performance becomes more theatrical. And it needs special material—it can include melodrama, literary things, musical things, or lights."[11]

Toward the end of the 1960s and into the early 1970s, Pink Floyd released three more new albums. *Ummagumma*, which came out in 1969, was a mix of live recordings and studio experiments. The album reached number five on the British charts. It also cracked the top one hundred in the United States at number seventy-four. This was the first time that a Pink Floyd record had landed on the U.S. charts.

Atom Heart Mother, released in 1970, did even better. It reached number one in the United Kingdom and number fifty-five in the United States. The title song, which was twenty-three minutes long, took up the entire first side of the album. The other side featured songs from Roger Waters, David Gilmour, and Rick Wright. There was also a "song" that featured the sounds of a man cooking and eating his breakfast and commenting on his actions. The album featured an image of a cow on the cover. In later years, both Gilmour and Waters would dismiss this album as not one of their best efforts.

During their concerts in the United States to promote *Atom Heart Mother*, Pink Floyd brought with them their new stereo system. They were joined onstage by a full orchestra and choir. After seeing a performance, one reviewer wrote,

"The great thing about Pink Floyd is that they can make the freaks sit down and listen."[12]

"There was less concern with Pink Floyd in the commercial potential of their music," Clifton said. "They were more interested in the connection that it could make with audiences."[13]

The band's *Meddle* album came out in 1971. It continued with the theme of long songs. The second side of this album was taken up entirely by one song, "Echoes." At twenty-three minutes long, it featured extended guitar and keyboard solos, and the sounds of seagulls and whales. Rick Wright described the creative process this way: "All of us [would be] in a rehearsal room, just sitting there thinking, playing, working out ideas to see if they went anywhere. It's a nice way to work, and I think, in a way, the most Floydian material we ever did came about that way."[14]

"I really am an inspiration person," Gilmour said. "I just wait to let inspiration strike. Obviously, I have written a lot of songs . . . where I have set down to try and write a song and sometimes that works quite well. Mostly, I have to say, it is from flashes of inspiration."[15]

As the 1970s began, Pink Floyd was thriving. The band seemed to have survived the loss of their former front man. But Syd Barrett was never far from the minds of his former band mates. They missed his creativity, his way of putting words together. And they understood the pressure Barrett

More than a movie!
An explosive cinema concert!

PINK FLOYD
An overwhelming full-volume Pink Floyd color experience!
An R. M. Production Directed by Adrian Maben

In the early 1970s, French director Adrian Maben filmed Pink Floyd while they performed in Pompeii in an ancient amphitheater.

must have felt to write hit songs, to be successful. They were feeling pressure as well.

"When you look at Pink Floyd's work, almost all of it . . . has definitely been under the shadow of Syd Barrett," said music professor Keith Clifton. "And Waters has talked about the fact that he drew on a lot of conversations that he had with Barrett in coming up with lyrics for later songs."[16]

The band members "did not necessarily want to replicate everything that they had done with Syd Barrett," Clifton said. "They wanted to sort of move on. But he was always definitely a presence, a shadow, if you will."[17]

Pink Floyd's next album reflected all the emotions the band members were going through at the time. The album was a concept album. This means that all the songs are linked to a single theme. Concept albums were not new; the Beatles had had a hit with their concept album *Sgt. Pepper's Lonely Hearts Club Band*.

But Pink Floyd's concept album would take the genre further. Technologically, graphically, and musically, it would reach new heights. The album would come to be known as perhaps the band's magnum opus, its greatest achievement. And it would launch the group from a band with a very devoted but relatively small number of fans into international superstardom.

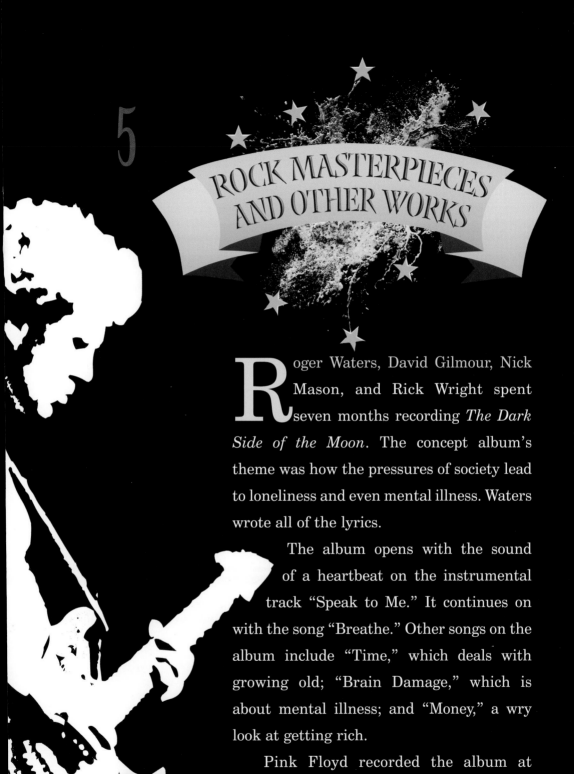

ROCK MASTERPIECES AND OTHER WORKS

Roger Waters, David Gilmour, Nick Mason, and Rick Wright spent seven months recording *The Dark Side of the Moon*. The concept album's theme was how the pressures of society lead to loneliness and even mental illness. Waters wrote all of the lyrics.

The album opens with the sound of a heartbeat on the instrumental track "Speak to Me." It continues on with the song "Breathe." Other songs on the album include "Time," which deals with growing old; "Brain Damage," which is about mental illness; and "Money," a wry look at getting rich.

Pink Floyd recorded the album at Abbey Road Studios, the London recording studio made famous by the Beatles. The studio engineer was Alan Parsons, who would go on to have a recording career of his own with the Alan Parsons Project. Parsons won a Grammy Award in 1973 for *Dark Side* for best engineered album.

Parsons used some of the most advanced technology of the day. Also, unusual sound effects were brought in to layer over the songs. For example, the sounds of coins and cash registers can be heard in the opening of "Money." Clock chimes ring throughout "Time."

"Alan Parsons had just been sent out to do a recording in a clock shop for the sound effects library," recalled David Gilmour. "He said, 'Listen, I just did all these things, I just did all these clocks,' and so we wheeled out his tape and listened to it and said, 'Great! Stick it on!'"[1]

"It felt like the whole band [was] working together," recalled Rick Wright. "It was a creative time. We were all very *open*."[2]

It was not just the songs that made the album so special, said Keith Clifton. The packaging of the album was also unique. For example, the black cover contained a single image. It was a prism with a beam of light shining through it. Also, "there were no lyrics, no indication of what the songs are," Clifton said, "just that strange prism. It was something that was pretty groundbreaking."[3]

As a concept album, *Dark Side* was meant to be listened

to from the beginning to the end, and not broken up into individual songs for radio play. Still, "Money" reached the top twenty on the U.S. charts. It was the only song on the album to do so.

"'Money' is a very unusual song," Clifton said, noting that it is in a different meter than most other rock songs. Meter is the basic rhythmical pattern of a song.

Dark Side was released in March 1973 and became an instant hit. A reviewer for *Rolling Stone* magazine called it "a fine album with a textural and conceptual richness that not only invites, but demands involvement. There is a certain grandeur here that exceeds mere musical melodramatics and is rarely attempted in rock." The reviewer also noted that the album "has flash—the true flash that comes from the excellence of a superb performance."[4]

Some listeners claimed that *Dark Side* had been created to be synchronized with the 1939 movie *The Wizard of Oz*. When the album and the movie were played at the same time, the movie scenes went along with the music and lyrics. But Pink Floyd band members said if this were, indeed, true, it was just a coincidence.

"The album's like a flower; it keeps opening," said one fan on the thirtieth anniversary of the release of *Dark Side*. "All these layers of sounds and the chords and the guitar lines . . . they [are] all like [a flower] and they move around you the way other . . . rock albums don't."[5]

While the Pink Floyd band members were happy the album had been so well received, they were surprised at its phenomenal success. Nick Mason said he believed *Dark Side* was so successful because the songs were "strong and powerful," and that the theme of the pressures of modern life "continues to capture people's imagination. . . . I think we all knew [it] was a very good record when we finished it," he said, "but I certainly had no real inkling of its commercial potential, and was as surprised as everyone else when it simply took off."[6]

After *Dark Side*, Pink Floyd switched from EMI to the Columbia record label. In January 1975, they returned to Abbey Road Studios to create another concept album. *Wish You Were Here* contains songs questioning the music industry's understanding of recording artists. The album also pays tribute to Syd Barrett with the title track and the instrumental "Shine On You Crazy Diamond." In an eerie coincidence, Barrett showed up at the studio while the band was recording this song. His former band members had not seen him or talked to him in many years. They did not recognize him at first: He had shaved his head and eyebrows, and had gained a lot of weight.

Bjorn Berkhout is a composer, cellist, and music professor at Loyola University in Chicago. He recalled the first time he heard *Wish You Were Here*. "I listened to the beginning and I needed to hear it all the way through," he said. "It was like listening to a Brahms symphony, [where] I had to start in the first movement and I had to listen all the way through to all four movements."[7]

"It was the same thing," with Pink Floyd, Berkhout said. "I had to start on side one, track one, and listen until . . . the end—because it was engaging. There was something about the music that suggested it was somehow one large expression, not a bunch of separate little songs. And I think that's what got me really, really hooked. For me, *Wish You Were Here* is Pink Floyd's grandest work," Berkhout said. "Everything about that album works."[8]

The album reached the number one spot on Billboard's pop album chart and stayed there for two weeks. To date, more than 12 million copies worldwide have been sold.

Pink Floyd followed *Wish You Were Here* with *Animals*, which was released in 1977. Another concept album, it divided society into dogs, pigs, and sheep. For their concert tours, the band utilized props such as a giant, inflatable flying pig. Some concerts were held in a baseball park in Anaheim, California. Up to fifty thousand people attended each show.

Animals was not as critically acclaimed as the two albums it followed. One reviewer called David Gilmour's guitar solos "thin" and "brittle." He also said, "The singing is more wooden than ever. The sound is more complex, but it lacks real depth; there's nothing to match the incredible intro to 'Dark Side of

the Moon.' . . . Floyd has turned bitter and morose."[9] However, *Animals* was another big seller for Pink Floyd.

The members of Pink Floyd had experienced great success. But the pressures of the business were affecting them. During one concert, an exhausted Waters got angry and spit on a fan in the front row.[10] Later, he began writing songs to come to terms with what he had done, and to deal with his feelings of isolation. These songs became Pink Floyd's next album.

The Wall, which was released in 1979, features lyrics written entirely by Waters. The theme of this two-disc album is loneliness and alienation. *The Wall* also was a symbol for the separation Pink Floyd felt from its audience as the band became more and more popular.

The Wall was number one on the Billboard Top 10 list for fifteen weeks. A song from that album, "Another Brick in the Wall (Part II)" hit the number one spot on the charts on March 22, 1980. It stayed there for four weeks. This was the only Pink Floyd single ever to land on the number one spot.

"Another Brick in the Wall (Part II)" is a song about feeling alienated in school. In fact, the white-led government in South Africa banned the song from radio play because black schoolchildren in that country were using the song to protest the inferior education they were receiving. When Waters wrote the song, he drew on his own unhappy childhood experiences. "It's not meant to be a blanket condemnation

of teachers everywhere, but the bad ones can really do people in—and there were some at my school who were just incredibly bad and treated the children so badly, just putting them down . . . all the time," Waters said. "Never encouraging them to do things, not really trying to interest them in anything, just trying to keep them quiet and still, and crush them into the right shape, so that they would go to university and 'do well.'"[11]

PINK FLOYD'S CONCERTS FOR THE WALL INCLUDED A WALL OF CARDBOARD BOXES ON STAGE BEHIND THEM. THE WALL WOULD COLLAPSE DURING THE HEIGHT OF THE CONCERT.

The song originally was intended to be a simple tune with one verse and chorus. However, Waters and Gilmour decided to add some young voices to get the school flavor. A recording engineer asked a music teacher at Islington Green School to bring some students to the studio to record a few tracks. The teacher chose about twelve students and with very little rehearsal, they began recording. The students sang the tracks several times to make it sound as though many more students were singing. The students received tickets to a Pink Floyd concert and a copy of the album, but no money.[12]

Other songs on *The Wall* included "Comfortably Numb" and "Hey You." The latter song "is a cry to the rest of the world . . . saying, hey, this isn't right," Waters said. "The basic idea of the whole thing really is that if you isolate yourself you decay."[13]

The Pink Floyd concerts for *The Wall* tour included a huge wall of cardboard boxes that collapsed during the climax of the performance.

In 1981, British director Alan Parker made a film of *The Wall*. It starred Bob Geldof and combined live action with animation. One reviewer wrote that the movie used flashbacks and hallucinations "to present a violent, disturbing insight into Pink, a burned-out rock star."[14]

"It was one of the most miserable experiences I've had working on a film, mostly because of Roger [Waters]," Parker said. "It was his miserable life that I was filming.

IN 1981, A MOVIE CALLED *THE WALL* WAS RELEASED.
THIS IS A SCENE FROM THE MOVIE.

The problem wasn't over creative differences, just a collision of egos."[15]

"I went to the movie when it came out," said professor Frank Felice. "I came away just going, 'Man, life is a bummer. Why would I like this band?'"[16]

"When I was in high school, I saw 'The Wall' at a theater, which was a pretty disturbing experience," said professor Keith Clifton. "But I have great respect for [Pink Floyd] as artists."[17]

Though *The Wall* was another hit for Pink Floyd, band members had experienced a lot of tension recording it. Indeed, Waters and Gilmour had been having creative differences for several years. "As productive as we were, we could have been making better records if Roger had been willing to back off a little bit, to be more open to other people's input," Gilmour once said.[18]

Waters was also battling with keyboardist Wright. He felt Wright was not contributing enough and had been slacking off for many years. Waters demanded that Wright be fired, and Wright left before the album was completed.

"I wasn't particularly happy with the band anyway." Wright said. "I'm in no way trying to put this man [Waters] down. I think he has great ideas. But he is an extremely difficult man to work with."[19]

The remaining members of Pink Floyd began recording another album, *The Final Cut*, in July 1982, and it was released in March 1983. Waters wrote all the lyrics on the album and dedicated it to his father, who had died during World War II. "As soon as I could talk, I was asking where my daddy was," Waters said.[20]

One reviewer called the album a "powerful protest against Evil with a capital 'E'—injustice, suffering, war, greed, cruelty."[21] The reviewer also said, "Fairly simple melodies are brilliantly embellished with rock electronics and sound effects augmented by an experimental 3-D audio process called

Holophonics. . . . It is a son's requiem for a lost father that is also a plea for peace and prosperity."[22]

The Final Cut hit the top spot on the U.K. album charts and reached the number six spot in the United States. But there would be no tour to promote this album. Waters and Gilmour had continued to clash throughout the months of recording. Gilmour said Waters "was just obsessed with the idea that I was being destructive and I didn't believe absolutely and completely in everything he did and said."[23]

"The sound and the music [of *The Final Cut*] didn't, in the majority, come from Roger," Gilmour also said. "The lyrics came from Roger—as did a lot of the motivation and a lot of great stuff. I wouldn't for a minute try to play down Roger's importance in our career, 'cause that would be unfair. But it would be just as unfair to play down the importance of all the other elements that make up Pink Floyd."[24]

In 1985, Waters announced that the band was over and he would make solo albums. He did not think that Gilmour and Mason would continue Pink Floyd without him—but Gilmour and Mason had other plans. They wanted to keep playing music as Pink Floyd. Waters sued to try to prevent Gilmour and Mason from using the band's name. "If one of us was going to be called Pink Floyd, it's me," Waters said.[25]

"Nobody else in the band could write lyrics," Waters also said. "David's written a couple of songs but they're nothing

special. I don't think Nick ever tried to write a lyric and Rick probably did in the very early days, but they were awful."[26]

The matter was eventually settled out of court. Mason and Gilmour could continue as Pink Floyd, and Waters received exclusive rights to some of the band's works. "They are now Pink Floyd. I'd rather they weren't—that's common knowledge," Waters said. "We went through a whole thing about that, and now it's over."[27]

Yet the hard feelings remained for the next several years. "What we miss of Roger is his drive, his focus, his lyrical brilliance—many things," Gilmour once said. "But I don't think any of us would say that music was one of the main ones . . . he's not a great musician."[28]

Responded Waters of Gilmour: "He is a great guitar player. But the idea . . . that he's somehow more musical than I am, is absolute . . . nonsense. It's an absurd notion."[29]

In October 1986, Mason and Gilmour began recording a new Pink Floyd album, *A Momentary Lapse of Reason*. Halfway through the project, keyboardist Rick Wright rejoined them. The album came out in 1987. Waters called it "a clever forgery,"[30] but other reviewers had more positive comments. One said the album "managed to rehash the group's trademark sound."[31] It was one of the top-ten selling albums of 1987.

Felice was playing in a band when *A Momentary Lapse of Reason* was released. "I remember very vividly the guys in my

band saying, 'Pink Floyd is Roger Waters; how can this even work [without him]?' But then I heard the album and I said, 'This is a Pink Floyd album. And it's an amazing album.'"[32]

Pink Floyd went on tour, and the band members were happy but surprised at the reception they received. "It's most peculiar," said drummer Nick Mason. "Pink Floyd are like one of those candles that never go out. You blow it, turn away, and the . . . thing is alight again."[33]

Yet the band members continued to be bitter about the breakup. "If you believe half of what Gilmour and Mason say . . . Waters is an arrogant dictatorial egomaniac hungry for all the credit," wrote David Fricke in *Rolling Stone* magazine. "If you believe half of what Waters says . . . they are lazy, greedy . . . hacking out a record and sleepwalking through a tour to build up a multimillion-dollar retirement nest egg."[34]

"None of them have any imagination," Waters also said about his former band mates. "They don't understand the work, they have no idea what any of it was about."[35]

In 1988, Pink Floyd released a live double album, *Delicate Sound of Thunder*. It reached number eleven on the Billboard 200 chart. Meanwhile, Waters launched a solo career. He released *Pros and Cons of Hitchhiking* in 1984 and *Radio KAOS* in 1987. When Waters went on tour to promote this latter album, it was a humbling experience. "Outside the major cities, we struggled to sell tickets," he said. "I remember playing Cincinnati the day after my ex-colleagues [Pink

Floyd] had sold out a 70,000 [capacity] football tickets. I was in an 8,000-capacity arena with about 1,500 people there."[36]

In 1990, Waters staged an elaborate production of *The Wall* in Berlin, Germany, shortly after the wall separating East Germany from West Germany was torn down and the country was reunified. More than two hundred fifty thousand people attended the show. Waters was joined onstage by singers Joni Mitchell, Bryan Adams, Van Morrison, Cyndi Lauper, and Sinead O'Connor, among others.

Rogers released another solo album, *Amused to Death*, in 1992. Two years later, Pink Floyd released a new album, *The Division Bell*. This album made it to the number one spot, attracting a new generation of fans. "I like Pink Floyd more than Pearl Jam," one twenty-year-old concertgoer admitted. "It's one thing my folks and I agree on. Kinda creepy, huh?"[37]

Said a seventeen-year-old fan: "The new bands just aren't as deep as Pink Floyd."[38]

Many music critics did not like the new album, however. "The band's talent and vision have always stayed a few steps ahead of their pretensions. Until now," one reviewer said. "Copycat songs . . . suggest an attempt to recapture the mood of their 1973 classic, 'The Dark Side of the Moon.' . . . So Pink Floyd strikes out, but at least they go down swinging."[39]

Another critic said that while *Dark Side* was a classic, "'The Division Bell' is anything but." He also said the "daring" sound effects on earlier Pink Floyd records now were old and predictable, and the lyrics were simplistic.[40]

This reviewer also noted that more than 3 million tickets had been sold for the U.S. tour and said, "The 16-year-olds at those concerts—eager like so many 16-year-olds before them to hear such alienated anthems as 'Money' and 'Another Brick in the Wall'—may be too young to notice or care about Waters' absence."[41]

Felice said, "Certainly, they were the best when they were together. And they were lesser when they're not." As an example, he cites Roger Waters's solo effort *Amused to Death*. He said the songs on the album "don't necessarily function well as good songs, but they're vehicles for the words." He also said that with the Gilmour-led Pink Floyd, "there are times when you wish the words weren't awkward."[42]

During a tour to promote *The Division Bell*, a magazine reporter asked Gilmour about his relationship with Waters. "I don't have one," Gilmour said. "I see his signature on bundles of royalty checks that are wheeled through my office from his office, and I sign my name next to his. That's about as close as we've got. I actually haven't seen or spoken to him since December '87, when we finally agreed to and signed the settlement deal."[43]

In May 1995, Pink Floyd released *Pulse*, a live, double album. It was recorded during the band's *Division Bell* tour the previous year. The album debuted at number one on the

Billboard 200 and to date, has sold almost 2 million copies in the United States. Pink Floyd was inducted into the Rock and Roll Hall of Fame in 1996, but Waters did not attend the ceremony.

Pulse would be Pink Floyd's last new album for awhile. For the next few years, Pink Floyd band members pursued individual interests. David Gilmour worked on material for solo albums and concentrated on his young family. Nick Mason pursued his love of auto racing. Roger Waters toured a bit and received favorable reviews. "Waters did just fine on his own . . . showing that, yes, he knows exactly what it is . . . that makes fans fanatical about his work," one reviewer wrote in 2000. "He bounded around the stage, clearly thrilled to be back on tour . . . Not that it wouldn't have been nice to have help from the old bandmates. As it was it took three guitarists to fill in for Gilmour."[44]

Then, in January 2002, Waters and Mason ran into each other while each was on vacation on the Caribbean island of Mustique. They enjoyed catching up with each other, and several months later, Waters called Mason and asked him to play a guest spot at his concert in Wembley Arena.[45] "I played on only one number . . . but the evening was fantastic," Mason recalled.[46]

A couple of years later, Mason's book, *Inside Out: The Personal History of Pink Floyd*, was published. During interviews to publicize the book, one reporter asked Mason if Pink

AFTER MANY YEARS OF NOT SEEING EACH OTHER, DAVID
GILMOUR (LEFT) AND ROGER WATERS REUNITED FOR THE
LIVE 8 CONCERTS.

Floyd would ever consider reuniting. "I could imagine doing
that," Mason said. "But I can't see Roger would want to. I
think David would have to feel extremely motivated to want to
get back to work."[47] Mason then added that perhaps if the
event were a charity concert, they might all agree.

Several months later, Bob Geldof began planning the
Live 8 concerts to benefit Africa. One of his assistants

mentioned hearing the comment Mason had made. Geldof
called Mason, Waters, and Gilmour. Mason and Waters said
yes, but Gilmour declined. So after not speaking to him for
several years, Waters called Gilmour—who thought about it
for a day and then said yes. Geldof then called Wright, who
also agreed. The reunion concert was on. For the first time
since 1981, Waters, Gilmour, Mason, and Wright would perform together as Pink Floyd.

"Any squabbles Roger and the band have had in the past
are so petty in this context, and if re-forming for this concert
will help focus attention then it's got to be worthwhile,"
Gilmour said.[48]

Later, Gilmour would say that his three youngest children
enjoyed watching him "up there [onstage] being a rock star,"
he said. "They now understand that I'm not just this bum who
lazes around the house, cooks them supper and takes them
to school."[49]

Gilmour's children were not the only ones who enjoyed
the reunion concert. Sales of some Pink Floyd records
increased by 1,000 percent after Live 8. Gilmour announced
that he would donate any of his profits that resulted from the
Live 8 concert to charities to help Africa. He urged others to
do the same. "If other artists feel like donating their extra
royalties to charity, perhaps then the record companies could
be persuaded to make a similar gesture and that would

be a bonus," he said. "This is money that should be used to save lives."[50]

There was one person, however, who did not enjoy the concert—because he did not see it. Syd Barrett, the founding father of Pink Floyd, was living as a recluse in Cambridge, England. He did not even own a television set.

The Pink Floyd appearance at Live 8 had been a great success and Waters, Gilmour, Mason, and Wright seemed to enjoy themselves. A few months later, they were inducted into the U.K. Music Hall of Fame. Was it too much to hope that the band would officially reunite?

On July 7, 2006, Syd Barrett died. Some fans left flowers at his home in

6

THE BAND MEMBERS TODAY

On July 7, 2006, former Pink Floyd front man Roger "Syd" Barrett died. He was sixty years old. Some reports said he had diabetes, a disease marked by high levels of sugar in the blood. Other reports said he had cancer of the pancreas. Barrett had remained reclusive to his death.

Peter Jenner was the original manager of Pink Floyd. He said he had heard a rumor that Barrett "seemed to feel that they [Pink Floyd] were still his band, and it was very hard to get through to him. So I don't know whether he fully accepted that he had left the band or what his position was."[1] However, Barrett's sister, Rosemary Breen, said Barrett was not mentally ill. She said her brother had spent the past several years gardening, listening to jazz music, and painting.[2]

"I can't tell you how sad I feel" about Barrett's death, said rock icon David Bowie. Bowie had recorded Barrett's song "Arnold Layne" back in the 1970s, and called Barrett a major inspiration. "The few times I saw him perform in London . . . during the '60s will forever be etched in my mind. He was so charismatic and such a startlingly original songwriter."[3]

"Syd was the guiding light of the early band line-up," the remaining members of Pink Floyd said in a statement released to the media. "He leaves a legacy which continues to inspire."[4]

"I think Syd leaves an extraordinary legacy because Floyd [is] famous all over the world," music producer Joe Boyd said. "The fact that nobody's really heard his voice or his guitar-playing doesn't really stop the fact that people revere him, and I think it's quite correct that they should."[5]

After Barrett's death, several fans wrote e-mail condolence messages to a British Broadcasting Company (BBC) Web site. One woman wrote that she had been a fan of Barrett's since Pink Floyd's first album, *The Piper at the Gates of Dawn*, was released. Barrett's "childlike quality came through in his songs, the words so simple but the meaning often diverse and complex," she wrote. She added that some of the words from his song, "Jugband Blues," which was included on Pink Floyd's *A Saucerful of Secrets* album, "always seemed like a cry for help."[6]

"My 6-year-old daughter, Emily, is named after one of his songs," wrote another fan. "Syd Barrett was a supernova of talent and creativity that burned energetically, brightly, and explosively for a very short time."[7]

Barrett was worth more than one million dollars when he died. He had been living comfortably, though simply, because of royalties he had been receiving from his songs. However, he had just a few possessions, including paintings he created. They were auctioned off; his family said the money would be used for art-education programs. Barrett "did his artworks and then destroyed them all, so very few of his originals exist," said auctioneer Martin Millard. "He would paint a picture, take a Polaroid of it, keep the photograph and destroy the original. We have absolutely no idea [why he did this], it just seemed to be his thing."[8] Millard also said Barrett's most recent work was painted six months before he died. It was a still life of lemons and green bottles on a shelf.

Barrett also left behind a scrapbook that included a magazine article on a 200-carat diamond. "We all like to think that there might be a link somewhere between this and 'the crazy diamond' himself," Millard said.[9] Barrett's other possessions included a couple of hand-painted bicycles, and some guitars and speakers.

The home in Cambridge that Barrett lived in was also sold. It is now part of the England Rocks! campaign, which is designed to attract visitors to the country. The campaign features a listing of landmarks that would appeal to tourists interested in British rock music history.

"Roger loved the peace and quiet" of his home, his sister, Rosemary Breen, said. "He put his stamp on the house with frequent redecoration, building his own furniture, changing doors." Breen noted that Barrett used the front rooms for drawing, painting, and writing notes about art history. In the back room, he listened to jazz music. "Upstairs he slept in all the bedrooms, deciding which one as the mood took him," Breen said.[10]

A few months after Barrett's death, David Gilmour released a tribute single. It featured two versions of "Arnold Layne," one sung by David Bowie and the other by Pink Floyd keyboardist Rick Wright. Gilmour later released a solo acoustic version of "Dark Globe." This was a song written by Barrett and included on the 1970 solo album *The Madcap Laughs*.

Almost a year after Barrett's death, a tribute concert was held at Barbican Centre in London. It featured top British performers singing Barrett's songs in front of psychedelic visuals. These visuals were created by people who had worked on early Pink Floyd light shows. But if there were any hopes the remaining members of Pink Floyd would reunite for the tribute concert, those hopes were dashed. David Gilmour, Nick Mason, and Rick Wright performed "Arnold Layne," the band's first hit, but Roger Waters did not join them. He played

his own song, "Flickering Flame." Gilmour, Mason, and Wright took the stage again for the finale, a performance of the single "Bike" from Pink Floyd's first album, *The Piper at the Gates of Dawn*. They were joined by all the other musicians who had participated in the tribute concert—all except for Waters. A few fans shouted, "Where's Roger?"[11]

At the time of Syd Barrett's death, the members of Pink Floyd had been active in music, though they were usually taking separate paths. In March 2006, David Gilmour released his third solo album, *On an Island*. Pink Floyd keyboardist Rick Wright was among those who played with Gilmour on the CD. Gilmour, then sixty years old, said his fingers did not move as fast as they once did, but he was comfortable playing at a slower pace. "He carves epic solos out of long, gracefully sustained notes," said one reviewer. "It's a way of playing that's been missing from rock for a long time."[12] Gilmour and Wright went on tour to promote the album. They included some Pink Floyd tunes in their concert performances.

A few months after Gilmour's solo album was released, Roger Waters and Nick Mason began a tour through Europe that eventually made its way to the United States. The tour included a performance of *The Dark Side of the Moon* in its entirety. Newspapers reported that tickets for some of the performances had sold so quickly that bids were being taken online for available seats. Some online tickets were selling as high as $4,600 each.[13]

NICK MASON ENJOYS COLLECTING AND DRIVING CARS. HE IS KNEELING NEXT TO HIS 1995 McLAREN F1 GTR.

"What I've noticed in the last year or so, playing it again and listening to it, is how relevant the lyrics are to an older generation," Mason said about *Dark Side*. "Even though we were in our 20s when we were working on it, the lyrics could have been written for 50-year-olds."[14]

A reviewer at one Waters concert said it felt like a Pink Floyd gig, complete with a large inflatable pig. This one had "Impeach Bush Now" and other political messages written on it. "Only at a concert filled with performances of Pink Floyd songs could a pig fly, and the floating swine made it feel like the real deal despite Waters being the only member of the band on stage," the reviewer wrote.[15]

Roger Waters also was reportedly working on a Broadway version of *The Wall*. "Now I can write in some laughs, notable by their absence in the movie," Waters said.[16] The Broadway production was spearheaded by Miramax films cofounder Harvey Weinstein and Sony Music chief Tommy Mottola. "When I first thought of bringing this event to Broadway, I knew I could not do it without the visionary talents of Roger Waters," Mottola said.[17]

In July 2006, the DVD collection of Pink Floyd's *Pulse* came out. It went to the top of the music DVD charts—not only in the United Kingdom and United States but also in Austria, Belgium, Holland, Ireland, Italy, and Norway. Said one reviewer, "Those who were too young or not interested enough to see Pink Floyd during what became its last tour will probably have to make do with 'Pulse.' The band members have implied in interviews that they will not tour again."[18]

Surprisingly to some, however, Waters said he would not rule it out. "I would see no negative to playing with those guys again," the former Pink Floyd bass player said. "If something cropped up in the future, I see no reason why not."[19]

Instead, it is Gilmour who did not want to tour, either as Pink Floyd with Waters, or Pink Floyd without Waters.[20] Promoters agreed that if the band were to get back together

for a reunion tour, it would generate a lot of excitement and record-shattering ticket sales. "Unless John Lennon and George Harrison [of the Beatles] were able to resurrect themselves from the dead, there is no bigger tour," said one promoter. "If you could put one and one together, it equals a zillion. If they do want to get together, I have a gigantic check for them."[21] Sadly, a reunion of all the band members will never happen. In September 2008, Richard Wright died of cancer. He was 65 years old.

Today, more than thirty years after it was first released, *The Dark Side of the Moon* remains near the top of *Billboard*'s album charts. "It's an appetite that doesn't seem to be sated," said Geoff Mayfield, *Billboard*'s director of charts.[22] *Dark Side* is also the third best-selling album of all time. One British magazine writer said *Dark Side* sold so many copies during its heyday that it was "virtually impossible that a moment went by without it being played somewhere on the planet."[23]

In a recent *Guitar World* magazine poll, readers named *Dark Side* the fifth greatest guitar album of all time. It ranked number one in an Australian poll of favorite albums. *Rolling Stone* magazine listed it as number forty-three among the five hundred greatest albums of all time.

"So much of what's on the album . . . is just about life, really, in its most boring aspect," said one Pink Floyd fan. "It's about . . . time, money; nothing really new or fresh or original, but maybe that's why it's so . . . universal . . . why so many alienated 16-year-olds are listening to it now probably as much as they were in the early '70s."[24]

Additionally, Pink Floyd's *The Wall* was listed by *Rolling Stone* magazine as number eighty-seven of the five hundred greatest albums. And in February 2007, *Spin* magazine named Pink Floyd as one of the fifty greatest bands of all time. "The music is as relevant as it was 30 years ago," said an *Entertainment Weekly* reviewer.[25]

Pink Floyd has been a major influence on several of today's musical performers. The group's songs have been covered by the Smashing Pumpkins and REM, among others. Jam bands Phish and moe. have covered the entire *Dark Side* album during their concerts. A group of reggae artists reworked *Dark Side* into *Dub Side of the Moon*. The executive producer of the album, Lem Oppenheimer, was a big fan of the album when he was a teen. He would play Side 2 every morning before he went to school.[26] Bands who specialize in genres as varied as hard rock, heavy metal, and blues have said Pink Floyd was their inspiration.

Los Angeles Lakers basketball star Vladimir Radmanovic once said he listened to the song "Shine on you Crazy Diamond," from *Wish You Were Here* to get ready for National Basketball Association playoff games. "It's not really an upbeat song, but it pumps me up for some reason," he said. "I also like 'Time' and 'Wish You Were Here.'"[27]

"New bands discover [Syd Barrett] all the time," said

ROGER WATERS
CONTINUES TO TOUR
AND IS REPORTEDLY
WORKING ON A
BROADWAY VERSION
OF *THE WALL*.

Tim Willis, who wrote a biography of Barrett. He also said that he was confident that "Arnold Layne" and "See Emily Play" would live forever as pop songs.[28]

So the band Pink Floyd may no longer be together, but their music lives on. Composer and cellist Bjorn Berkhout wrote a graduate school thesis on the music of Pink Floyd. "If you look at how the music of Pink Floyd is working structurally and sonically . . . you unlock their expression," he said. "And you can walk away from a work like 'The Wall' and instead of just having kind of a vague idea of what this is all about, you know exactly why they made the decision to use that sound at that moment. And you get a much more intense experience listening to the music. Because suddenly you realize how much depth of expression this music really has."[29]

The music of Pink Floyd "is so compelling," Berkhout also said. "It works. It's rewarding to listen to, it's beautiful to listen to, it's emotional to listen to. So even without knowing all the issues behind it, it works on its own right."[30]

TIMELINE

1943—Rick Wright is born in London, England, on July 28; Roger Waters is born in Great Bookham, England, on September 6.

1944—Nick Mason is born in Birmingham, England, on January 27.

1946—Waters's father, Eric Fletcher Waters, dies during the battle of Anzio, Italy, in January; Roger "Syd" Barrett is born in Cambridge, England, on January 6; David Gilmour is born in Cambridge on March 6.

1962—Waters, Mason, and Wright individually enroll at Regent Street Polytechnic School in London to study architecture; Gilmour and Barrett meet at Cambridge College of Arts and Technology, where they both are students.

1964—Barrett moves to London to attend the Camberwell School of Art.

1963–1965—Barrett, Waters, Mason, and Wright form a band with Bob Klose and Chris Dennis.

1965—Dennis and Klose leave the band. Barrett meets up with Gilmour in France, where Gilmour is

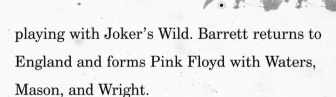

playing with Joker's Wild. Barrett returns to England and forms Pink Floyd with Waters, Mason, and Wright.

1965–1967—Pink Floyd lands gigs in "underground" clubs throughout London. Barrett's mental health begins to deteriorate.

1967—Pink Floyd releases two singles and its first album, *The Piper at the Gates of Dawn*. Band begins to tour, but Barrett is increasingly unreliable and difficult to deal with.

1968—Barrett leaves the band and is replaced by David Gilmour; the band's second album, *A Saucerful of Secrets*, is released.

1969–1971—Pink Floyd releases three more albums.

1970—Barrett releases two solo albums.

1973—Pink Floyd becomes an international sensation with the release of their concept album *The Dark Side of the Moon*.

1975—Pink Floyd's second concept album, *Wish You Were Here*, is released.

1977—*Animals* is released.

1979—Wright leaves Pink Floyd before the band completes its latest album, *The Wall*.

1980—After living in London for several years, Barrett returns to his family's home in Cambridge; the Pink Floyd song "Another Brick in the Wall (Part II)" hits number one and remains in the top spot for four weeks.

1981—A film version of *The Wall* stars the Boomtown Rats' Bob Geldof.

1983—*The Final Cut* is released.

1985—Waters announces that Pink Floyd is over and he will make solo albums, then battles with Gilmour and Mason over the right to use the Pink Floyd name. Gilmour and Mason win.

1986—Gilmour and Mason are joined by Wright and release *A Momentary Lapse of Reason*.

1987—Waters's second solo album, *Radio KAOS*, is released.

1990–1992—Waters goes on tour and releases his third solo album.

1994—Pink Floyd releases *The Division Bell*, which makes it to the number one spot on the charts.

1995—Pink Floyd releases a live, double album, *Pulse*. It will be the last new album they release.

1996—Pink Floyd is inducted into the Rock and Roll Hall of Fame; Waters is a no-show.

2002—Waters and Mason meet unexpectedly while on vacation.

2004—Mason publishes a book, *Inside Out: The Personal History of Pink Floyd*.

2005—Waters, Gilmour, Mason, and Wright reunite for the Live 8 concert in Hyde Park, London. A few months later, the group is inducted into the U.K. Music Hall of Fame.

2006—Gilmour releases his third solo album; former Pink Floyd front man Roger "Syd" Barrett dies at the age of sixty.

2007—A tribute concert is held for Barrett. Gilmour, Mason, and Wright perform together as Pink Floyd; Waters also performs but as a solo act.

2008—Richard Wright dies of cancer at the age of sixty-five.

DISCOGRAPHY

**Pink Floyd with Syd Barrett, Nick Mason, Roger
Waters, Rick Wright**

The Piper at the Gates of Dawn, 1967

**Pink Floyd with Syd Barrett, Nick Mason, Roger
Waters, Rick Wright, David Gilmour**

A Saucerful of Secrets, 1968

**Pink Floyd with Nick Mason, Roger Waters, Rick
Wright, David Gilmour**

Ummagumma, 1969

Atom Heart Mother, 1970

Meddle, 1971

The Dark Side of the Moon, 1973

Wish You Were Here, 1975

Animals, 1977

The Wall, 1979

**Pink Floyd with Nick Mason, Roger Waters, David
Gilmour**

The Final Cut, 1983

Pink Floyd with Nick Mason, David Gilmour, Rick Wright

A Momentary Lapse of Reason, 1987

Delicate Sound of Thunder, 1988

The Division Bell, 1994

Pulse, 1995

CONCERT TOURS

November 1967—First tour of the United States; *The Jimi Hendrix Experience*

July 1968—*A Saucerful of Secrets*

May 1969—*The Man/The Journey*

September 1970—*Atom Heart Mother World Tour*

October 1971—*Meddle*

March 1973—*The Dark Side of the Moon*

November 1974—*British Winter Tour*

April 1975—*Wish You Were Here*

January 1977—*Animals*

February 1980—*The Wall*

September 1987—*A Momentary Lapse of Reason*

March 1994—*The Division Bell*

GLOSSARY

acoustic—A musical instrument that has not been electronically modified.

activist—Someone who takes an active role in a political or social cause.

amenities—Things that provide convenience or enjoyment.

architecture—The practice of designing and building structures.

auditory—Related to hearing.

cover—A different version of a song.

flashback—To experience in the mind a past incident as though it were happening again.

gig—A job that is performed for a short period of time.

glorify—To make something seem better than it really is.

hallucinations—An unfounded or mistaken perception.

impromptu—Unplanned.

jam—To improvise while playing music with others.

juxtaposition—To be positioned side by side.

lyrics—Words to a song.

pathologist—Doctor who studies how diseases change the body.

psychedelic—Distorted images and sounds to affect perceptions.

quintessential—Best representation of something.

reclusive—Withdrawn from society.

schizophrenia—A mental illness that affects perceptions of reality.

PINK FLOYD
THE ROCK BAND

Chapter Notes

Chapter 1. "The Greatest Rock Concert Ever"

1. Matthew Schofield, "Live 8 Concerts Seek to Change Policies of Leading Countries," Knight-Ridder/Tribune News Service, July 1, 2005, <http://elibrary.bigchalk.com> (June 30, 2007).

2. Randy Lewis and Vanora Bennett, "Aid for Africa; Start to Make It Better, Live 8 Urges; Nearly 1 Million Attend 10 Concerts Worldwide Aimed at Getting G-8 to Address African Poverty," *Los Angeles Times*, July 3, 2005, p. A–1.

3. Jill Lawless, Associated Press, "1 Million Fans Gather Across Globe for Live 8 Concert; Shows in Philadelphia and London Draw Largest Crowds," *Allentown Morning Call*, July 3, 2005, p. A–7.

4. "Pink Floyd Set Squabbles Aside to Reunite for London Live 8 Concert," *Agence France-Presse English*, July 2, 2005, <http://elibrary.bigchalk.com> (June 30, 2007).

5. Nick Mason, *Inside Out: A Personal History of Pink Floyd* (San Francisco, Calif.: Chronicle Books, 2004), p. 344.

6. Ibid.

7. Jim DeRogatis, "Live 8 Takes Off; Ten Simultaneous Concerts Push for an End to Africa's

Poverty: Naive, Sure, But the World Sings for a Day," *Chicago Sun-Times*, July 4, 2005, p. 30.

    8. Mike Watkinson and Pete Anderson, *Crazy Diamond: Syd Barrett and the Dawn of Pink Floyd* (London, England: Omnibus Press, 2006), p. 164.

    9. Ibid., p. 121.

    10. Ibid., p. 163.

Chapter 2. "One of the Saddest Stories in Rock 'n' Roll"

    1. Mike Watkinson and Pete Anderson, *Crazy Diamond: Syd Barrett and the Dawn of Pink Floyd* (London, England: Omnibus Press, 2006), p. 140.

    2. Ibid., p. 13.

    3. Ibid., p. 27.

    4. Toby Manning, *The Rough Guide to Pink Floyd* (New York: Rough Guides, an imprint of Penguin Books, 2006), p. 15.

    5. Ibid., p. 73.

    6. Ibid., p. 18.

    7. "NIDA InfoFacts: LSD," National Institute on Drug Abuse, n.d., <http://www.nida.nih.gov/Infofacts/LSD.html> (July 18, 2007).

    8. Ibid.

    9. Cliff Jones, "Wish You Were Here," *Mojo*, September 1996, <http://www.pink-floyd.org/artint/mojose96.htm> (July 29, 2007).

10. "Interview: Joe Boyd, Record Producer and Author of the New Memoir 'White Bicycles,' on Producing Albums and Festivals in the '60s," *Fresh Air*, *National Public Radio*, airdate March 20, 2007.

11. Personal interview with Frank Felice, June 22, 2007.

12. Ibid.

13. "Syd Barrett (Obituary)," *The Economist*, July 22, 2006, p. 83.

14. Manning, p. 72.

15. Clark Collis, "Syd Barrett 1946–2006," *Entertainment Weekly*, July 21, 2006, p. 17.

16. Manning, p. 75.

17. Graham Fuller, "The Color of Floyd," *Interview*, July 1994, p. 20.

18. Manning, p. 122.

19. Ibid., p. 123.

20. Chet Flippo, "After a Record-Breaking Decade on the Charts, Pink Floyd's David Gilmour Tries a Solo Tour," *People Weekly*, March 12, 1984, p. 103.

21. Manning, p. 90.

22. "Musicians Remember Their First Instrument," BBC News, December 18, 2004, <http://news.bbc.co.uk/2/hi/uk_news/4107033.stm> (June 1, 2007).

23. Nick Mason, *Inside Out: A Personal History of Pink Floyd* (San Francisco, Calif.: Chronicle Books, 2004), p. 9.

24. Ibid.

25. Irwin Stambler, *The Encyclopedia of Pop, Rock, and Soul* (New York: St. Martin's Press, 1989), p. 522.

Chapter 3. Leonard's Lodgers

1. Mike Watkinson and Pete Anderson, *Crazy Diamond: Syd Barrett and the Dawn of Pink Floyd* (London, England: Omnibus Press, 2006), p. 29.

2. Bruno MacDonald, ed., *Pink Floyd: Through the Eyes of . . . the Band, its Fans, Friends and Foes* (New York: Da Capo Press, 1996), p. 312.

3. Watkinson and Anderson, p. 31.

4. MacDonald, p. 11.

5. Darrin Foh, "Syd Barrett 1946–2006, Riffs: Tribute," *Guitar Player*, November 2006, p. 40.

6. "Musician Syd Barrett Dies at Age 60," *All Things Considered*, National Public Radio, July 11, 2006.

7. Watkinson and Anderson, p. 45.

8. Ibid., p. 50.

9. Adam Bernstein, "Syd Barrett: Troubled Pink Floyd Frontman," *The Washington Post*, July 12, 2006, p. B–1.

10. Clark Collis, "Legacy: Syd Barrett 1946–2006," *Entertainment Weekly*, July 21, 2006, p. 17.

11. Nick Mason, *Inside Out: A Personal History of Pink Floyd* (San Francisco, Calif.: Chronicle Books, 2004), p. 87.

12. John Harris, *The Dark Side of the Moon: The Making of the Pink Floyd Masterpiece* (New York: Da Capo Press, 2005), p. 35.

13. Ibid., p. 56.

14. "The Stars Who Disappeared: Former Big Country Singer Stuart Adamson Has Been Found Dead After Being Reported Missing. BBC News Online Remembers Other Rock Stars Who Have Walked Away From the Spotlight," BBC News, December 17, 2001, <http://news.bbc.co.uk/2/hi/entertainment/1716201.stm> (June 18, 2007).

15. Mason, p. 97.

16. MacDonald, p. 12.

17. Harris, p. 45.

18. Mason, pp. 102–103.

19. Harris, p. 46.

Chapter 4. A Good Time for Rock

1. Norm N. Nite, *Rock On Almanac: The First Four Decades of Rock 'n' Roll* (New York: HarperCollins, 1992), p. 183.

2. Nick Mason, *Inside Out: A Personal History of Pink Floyd* (San Francisco, Calif.: Chronicle Books, 2004), p. 107.

3. Personal interview with Frank Felice, June 22, 2007.

4. Personal interview with Keith Clifton, July 18, 2007.

5. "Analysis: History and Cultural Impact of the

Electric Guitar," *National Public Radio, Talk of the Nation*, Juan Williams, host, March 14, 2000.

6. "Barrett's 'Extraordinary Legacy,'" BBC News, July 11, 2006, <http://news.bbc.co.uk/2/hi/entertainment/5170028.stm> (June 19, 2007).

7. Mason, p. 107.

8. Personal interview with Bjorn Berkhout, June 27, 2007.

9. John Harris, *The Dark Side of the Moon: The Making of the Pink Floyd Masterpiece* (New York: Da Capo Press, 2005), p. 57.

10. Personal interview with Keith Clifton, July 18, 2007.

11. Irwin Stambler, *The Encyclopedia of Pop, Rock and Soul* (New York: St. Martin's Press, 1989), p. 523.

12. Ibid.

13. Personal interview with Keith Clifton, July 18, 2007.

14. Bruno MacDonald, ed., *Pink Floyd: Through the Eyes of . . . the Band, its Fans, Friends and Foes* (New York: Da Capo Press, 1996), p. 13.

15. "David Gilmour in Concert," BBC Radio, May 29, 2006, <http:www.bbc.co.uk/radio2/events/davidgilmour/interview.shtml> (June 19, 2007).

16. Personal interview with Keith Clifton, July 18, 2007.

17. Ibid.

Chapter 5. Rock Masterpieces and Other Works

1. Tim Morse, *Classic Rock Stories* (New York: St. Martin's Griffin, 1998), p. 44.

2. John Harris, *The Dark Side of the Moon: The Making of the Pink Floyd Masterpiece* (New York: Da Capo Press, 2005), pp. 9–10.

3. Personal interview with Keith Clifton, July 18, 2007.

4. Loyd Grossman, "A Review of Dark Side of the Moon," *Rolling Stone*, May 24, 1973, <www.pink-floyd.org/artint/118.htm> (July 29, 2007).

5. "Profile: Pink Floyd's 'The Dark Side of the Moon' Still Popular 30 Years After Its Original Release," *All Things Considered*, National Public Radio, May 1, 2003.

6. Nick Mason, *Inside Out: A Personal History of Pink Floyd* (San Francisco, Calif.: Chronicle Books, 2004), pp. 186–187.

7. Personal interview with Bjorn Berkhout, June 27, 2007.

8. Ibid.

9. Frank Rose, "Review of Animals," *Rolling Stone*, March 24, 1977, <www.pink-floyd.org/artint/116.htm> (July 29, 2007).

10. Fred Bronson, *The Billboard Book of Number 1 Hits* (New York: Billboard Books, an imprint of Watson-Guptill, 2003), p. 523.

11. Morse, p. 134.

12. "A Suit Against Pink Floyd," *The Biz*, Cable News Network, December 1, 2004, <http://elibrary.bigchalk.com/libweb/elib/do/document?set=search&groupid+1requestid=1> (December 3, 2006).

13. Morse, p. 87.

14. "Pink Floyd The Wall," *Magill's Survey of Cinema*, June 15, 1995, <http://elibrary.bigchalk.com/libweb/elib/do/document?set=search&groupid+1requestid=1> (December 3, 2006).

15. Sunny Lee, "Sonic Youthquake: Pink Floyd The Wall Shook the Foundations of the Pop Movie Musical When It Opened 19 Years Ago," *Entertainment Weekly*, August 10, 2001, p. 78.

16. Personal interview with Frank Felice, June 22, 2007.

17. Personal interview with Keith Clifton, July 18, 2007.

18. Bruno MacDonald, ed., *Pink Floyd: Through the Eyes of . . . the Band, its Fans, Friends and Foes* (New York: Da Capo Press, 1996), p. 7.

19. Ibid., p. 14.

20. Harris, p. 53.

21. "The Final Cut," *People Weekly*, May 9, 1983, p. 22.

22. Ibid.

23. Robin Denselow, "The Floyd's Tour de Force,"

The Guardian, July 22, 1988, <www.pink-floyd.org/ artint/6.htm> (July 29, 2007).

24. Graham Fuller, "The Color of Floyd," *Interview*, July 1994, p. 20.

25. MacDonald, pp. 4–5.

26. "One Giant Step for Pink Floyd," *The Washington Post*, April 28, 1993, <www.pink-floyd. org/artint/80.htm> (July 29, 2007).

27. Guy Garcia, "Waters Still Runs Deep," *People Weekly*, October 26, 1992, p. 166.

28. Harris, p. 13.

29. Ibid.

30. MacDonald, p. 15.

31. Guy Garcia, "The Band That Wouldn't Die: Twenty Years After Its Classic Album and a Decade Since Its Leader Left, Pink Floyd Has a Hit New Record. It's Terrible," *Time*, May 30, 1994, <http:// elibrary.bigchalk.com/libweb/elib/do/document?set= search&groupid+1requestid=1> (December 3, 2006).

32. Personal interview with Frank Felice, June 22, 2007.

33. Robin Denselow, "The Floyd's Tour de Force," *The Guardian*, July 22, 1988, <www.pink-floyd. org/artint/6.htm> (July 29, 2007).

34. MacDonald, p. 5.

35. Ibid.

36. Hugh Fielder and Bradley Bambarger,

"Waters to Tour 'In the Flesh'" *Billboard*, July 10, 1999, p. 1.

37. "Pink Floyd's Retrogressive Progression," *USA Today*, 1994, <www.pinkfloyd-co.com/band/interviews/grp/grpUSA.html> (July 23, 2007).

38. Ibid.

39. David Hiltbrand, "The Division Bell," *People Weekly*, April 18, 1994, p. 28.

40. Guy Garcia, "The Band That Wouldn't Die: Twenty Years After Its Classic Album and a Decade Since Its Leader Left, Pink Floyd Has a Hit New Record. It's Terrible," *Time*, May 30, 1994, <http://elibrary.bigchalk.com/libweb/elib/do/document?set=search&groupid+1requestid=1> (December 3, 2006).

41. Ibid.

42. Personal interview with Frank Felice, June 22, 2007.

43. Graham Fuller, "The Color of Floyd," *Interview*, July 1994, p. 20.

44. Mark Brown, "Roger Waters Plays Fine Show Without His Pink Floyd Mates," *Denver Rocky Mountain News*, July 4, 2000, <http://elibrary.big chalk.com/libweb/elib/do/document?set=search&groupid+1requestid=1> (December 3, 2006).

45. Mason, p. 340.

46. Ibid.

47. Ibid.

48. "Pink Floyd Set Squabbles Aside to Reunite

for London Live 8 Concert," *Agence France-Presse English*, July 2, 2005, <http://elibrary.bigchalk.com> (June 30, 2007).

49. Lorraine Ali, "Bright Side of the Moon: Forget That Black Outfit—David Gilmour Has Mellowed," *Newsweek*, March 13, 2006, p. 60.

50. Canadian Press/Associated Press, "Dion Booing Aside, Cohl Loved Barrie Show; And World-Wide Live 8 Concert Went So Well, Pink Floyd Sales Rocketed by 1,343 Percent," *Kitchener Waterloo Record*, July 7, 2005.

Chapter 6. The Band Members Today

1. "Syd Barrett Dies Age 60: Pink Floyd Legend Passes Away at Home," BBC 6 Music, July 11, 2006, <www.bbc.co.uk/6music/news/20060711_syd.shtml> (June 19, 2007).

2. "Syd Barrett 1946–2006," *Guitar Player*, November 2006, p. 40.

3. "Pink Floyd's Barrett Dies Aged 60: Syd Barrett, One of the Original Members of Legendary Rock Group Pink Floyd, Has Died at the Age of 60 From Complications Arising From Diabetes," BBC News, July 11, 2006, <http://news.bbc.co.uk/2/hi/entertainment/5169344.stm> (June 19, 2007).

4. Kevin Owens, "Passing Notes," *Guitar Player*, October 2006, p. 48.

5. "Barrett's 'Extraordinary Legacy': Joe Boyd—One of the Pivotal Figures of the 1960s Rock

Scene—Offers His Memories of Pink Floyd Founding Member Syd Barrett, Who Has Died Aged 60," BBC News, July 11, 2006, <http://news.bbc.co.uk/2/hi/ entertainment/5170028.stm> (June 19, 2007).

6. "Syd Barrett Dies Age 60: Pink Floyd Legend Passes Away at Home," BBC 6 Music, July 11, 2006, <www.bbc.co.uk/6music/news/20060711_syd.shtml> (June 19, 2007).

7. Ibid.

8. "People Like You: Shine On You Crazy Diamond," *BBC*, September 19, 2006, <http://www .bbc.co.uk/cambridgeshire/contents/articles/2006/09/ 19/syd_barrett_sept2006> (June 19, 2007).

9. Ibid.

10. "Syd Barrett's Home on the Market," *BBC News*, September 11, 2006, <news.bbc.co.uk/2/hi/ uk_news/England/cambridgeshire/5335494.stm> (July 29, 2007).

11. "Floyd Play at Barrett Tribute Gig," *BBC News*, May 11, 2007, <http://news.bbc.co.uk/2/hi/ entertainment/6643779.stm> (July 29, 2007).

12. "Former Pink Floyd Guitarist Releases Solo Album," *All Things Considered*, National Public Radio, March 7, 2006.

13. "Marketplace Report: Auctioning Off Hot Tickets," *Day to Day*, National Public Radio, May 22, 2006.

14. Mike Snider, "Pink Floyd Keeps Its 'Pulse' Racing," *Calgary Herald*, October 3, 2006, <http://

PINK FLOYD THE ROCK BAND

Release," *All Things Considered*, National Public Radio, May 1, 2003.

25. "Wish You Were There?" *Entertainment Weekly*, July 14, 2006, p. 80.

26. "Review: Reggae Version of the Classic Pink Floyd Album 'Dark Side of the Moon' Called 'Dub Side of the Moon,'" *All Things Considered*, National Public Radio, March 23, 2003.

27. "What Songs Get You Ready?" *USA Weekend*, April 20–22, 2007, p. 30.

28. "Pink Floyd's Barrett Dies Aged 60," *BBC News*, <http://news.bbc.co.uk/2/hi/entertainment/5169344.stm> (June 19, 2007).

29. Personal interview with Bjorn Berkhout, June 27, 2007.

30. Ibid.

FURTHER READING

Edward, Herman. *Pink Floyd*. Broomall, Penn.: Mason Crest Publishers, 2007.

Feinstein, Stephen. *The 1970s from Watergate to Disco*. Berkeley Heights, N.J.: Enslow Publishers, Inc., 2006.

Hayes, Malcolm. *1970s: Turbulent Times*. (20th Century Music series.) Milwaukee, Wisc.: Gareth Stevens Pub., 2002.

Manning, Toby. *The Rough Guide to Pink Floyd*. New York: Rough Guides, 2006.

Pink Floyd. *Pink Floyd Guitar Tab Anthology*. Warner Brothers, 2002.

Schaefer, A.R. *Forming a Band*. Mankato, Minn.: Capstone High-Interest Books, 2004.

INTERNET ADDRESSES

Pink Floyd
<http://www.pinkfloyd.com>

Pink Floyd Online
<http://www.pinkfloydonline.com>

INDEX